EMTs Help Us

W9-AFH-591

Aaron R. Murray

Enslow Elementary

an imprint of

Enslow Publishers, Inc.

40 Industrial Road
Box 398
Berkeley Heights, NJ 07922
USA

http://www.enslow.com

Enslow Elementary, an imprint of Enslow Publishers, Inc.
Enslow Elementary® is a registered trademark of Enslow Publishers, Inc.

Copyright © 2013 by Enslow Publishers, Inc.
All rights reserved.

No part of this book may be reproduced by any means
without the written permission of the publisher.

Library of Congress Cataloging-in-Publication Data
Murray, Aaron R.
  EMTs help us / Aaron R. Murray.
      p. cm. — (All about community helpers)
  Includes index.
  Summary: "Introduces pre-readers to simple concepts about EMTs using short sentences and
repetition of words"— Provided by publisher.
  ISBN 978-0-7660-4050-2
  1. Emergency medical technicians—Juvenile literature. 2. Emergency medicine—Juvenile literature.
I. Title.
  RC86.5.M87 2013
  616.02'5—dc23
                              2011031045
Future editions
Paperback ISBN 978-1-4644-0059-9
ePUB ISBN 978-1-4645-0966-7
PDF ISBN 978-1-4646-0966-4

Printed in the United States of America
032013 Lake Book Manufacturing, Inc., Melrose Park, IL
10 9 8 7 6 5 4 3 2

To Our Readers: We have done our best to make sure all Internet Addresses in this book were active
and appropriate when we went to press. However, the author and the publisher have no control over and
assume no liability for the material available on those Internet sites or on other Web sites they may link
to. Any comments or suggestions can be sent by e-mail to comments@enslow.com or to the address on
the back cover.

♻ Enslow Publishers, Inc., is committed to printing our books on recycled paper. The paper in every
book contains 10% to 30% post-consumer waste (PCW). The cover board on the outside of each book
contains 100% PCW. Our goal is to do our part to help young people and the environment too!

Photo Credits: iStockphoto.com: © Bryan Myhr, p. 3 (emergency), © Craig Stocks, p. 10; Larry
St. Pierre/Shutterstock.com, p. 8; Shutterstock.com, pp. 1, 3 (ambulance, hospital), 4, 6, 12, 14, 16,
18, 20, 22.

Cover Photo: Shutterstock.com

Note to Parents and Teachers
Help pre-readers get a jump start on reading. These lively stories introduce simple concepts with
repetition of words and short simple sentences. Photos and illustrations fill the pages with color and
effectively enhance the text. Free Educator Guides are available for this series at www.enslow.com.
Search for the *All About Community Helpers* series name.

Contents

Words to Know

ambulance emergency   hospital

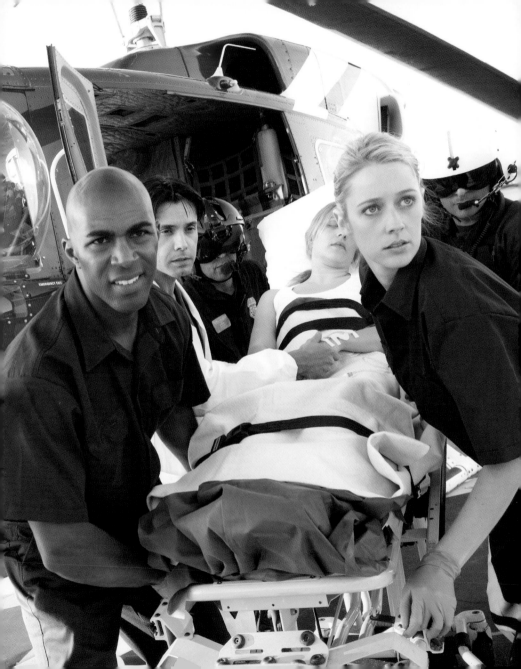

EMTs help people who are hurt.

EMTs help people who are sick, too.

**EMTs help
in an emergency.**

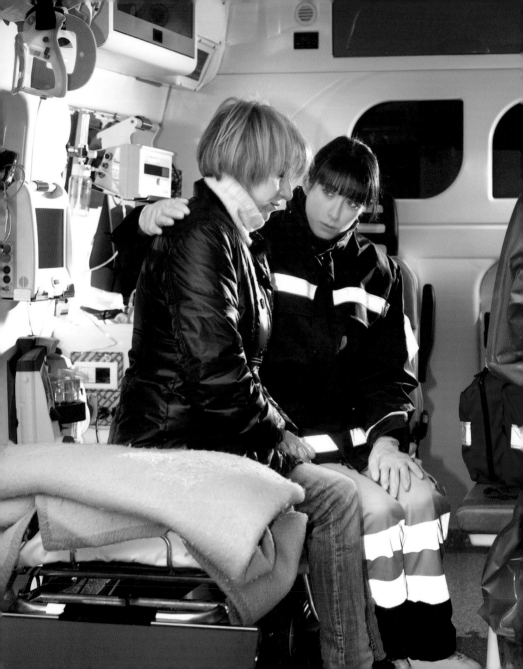

EMTs take care of
the hurt person.

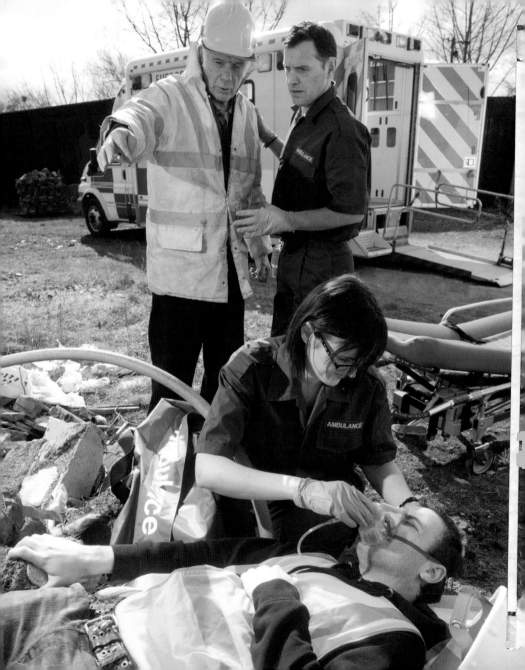

EMTs use a lot of tools.

EMTs call a doctor at the hospital.

EMTs tell the doctor to be ready to help.

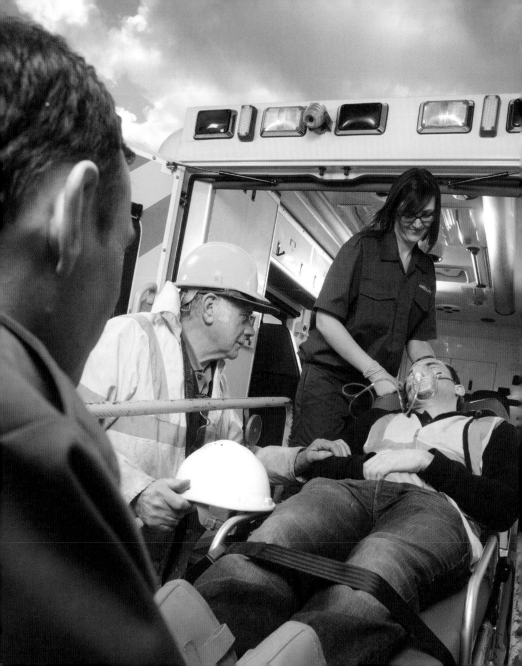

EMTs put the hurt person in an ambulance.

EMTs drive to the hospital.

The ambulance
lights flash.
"Move out of
the way!"

EMTs bring the hurt person into the hospital.

EMTs save lives.

Do you want to
help save lives?

You may want to
be an EMT.

Read More

Nelson, Kristin L. *EMTs*. Minneapolis, Minn.: Lerner Publishing Group, 2005.

Randolph, Joanne. *Ambulances*. New York: PowerKids Press, 2008.

Rau, Dana Meachen. *EMTs*. Tarrytown, N.Y.: Benchmark Books, 2008.

Web Sites

9-1-1 for Kids
<http://www.911forkids.com/>

NIEHS Kids' Pages
<http://kids.niehs.nih.gov/>

Index

Guided Reading Level: **C**
Guided Reading Leveling System is based on the guidelines recommended by Fountas and Pinnell.

Word Count: 82